ROAD SIGNS AND HOBO MARKS

Lois Parker Edstrom

ACKNOWLEDGMENTS

Grateful acknowledgment is made to the editors of the following publications in which these poems first appeared.

"Flight Path," Appears in *Glint,* MoonPath Press, 2019

"Moon Glow of Bone," First Place, Poetry Society of New Hampshire, 2012; Published in *Poet's Touchstone*, 2012

"Song for the Road," Tall Grass Writer's Guild, *Black and White Anthology*, 2015.

"Sourdough," *Sandy River Review*, 2016

"The Shape of Longing," Appears in *Night Beyond Black*, MoonPath Press, 2016

"Wings of Morning," Appears on cover of *Island of Faith, Sea of Grace*, 2013

"Yellowstone Park, 1948," *Through a Distant Lens,* Write Wing Publishing, 2014

"Wellington Train Disaster," Finalist Mississippi Valley Writing Contest (Midwest Writing Center) Published in *Off Channel* anthology, 2010

A special thanks to Rev. Tom Sutherland who initiated the conversation about hobo symbols that captured my imagination.

Thanks also to Rev. Billy Strayhorn whose life experience inspired the poem, *Extended Family*.

I'm grateful to Teresa Wiley, Diane Stone, and Sheryl Clough for their skillful reading, insightful suggestions, and unfailing friendship.

Thanks to Evan Edstrom who provided the images of hobo marks which appear in this book, and to Corey Cox who, with Teresa Wiley, made available a beautiful mountain retreat in which a good portion of this collection was written.

As always, love in abundance and thanks to my family and dear friends who are a constant source of inspiration.

In Memory of My Father
Cleve Jonathan Parker

Contents

HOBO MARKS

During the Great Depression hobos, who traveled to find work, developed a system of symbols, a unique code, which they chalked on fence posts, gates, homes, and various buildings to guide others who would follow.

HOBO MARKS

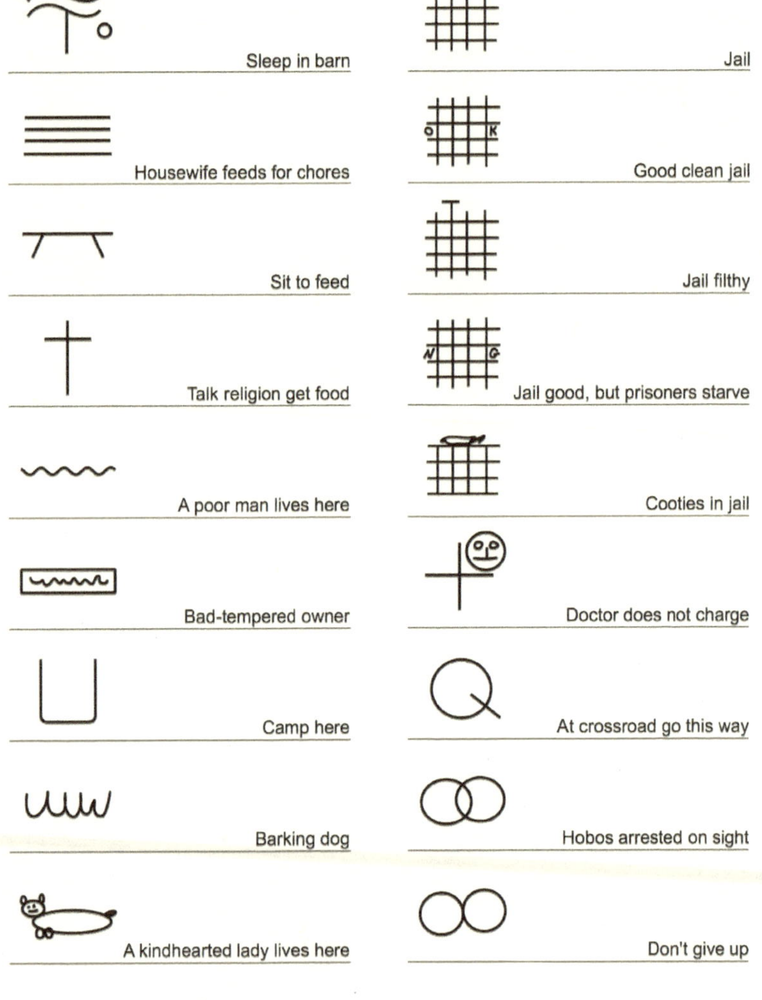

Sleep in barn
Housewife feeds for chores
Sit to feed
Talk religion get food
A poor man lives here
Bad-tempered owner
Camp here
Barking dog
A kindhearted lady lives here
Jail
Good clean jail
Jail filthy
Jail good, but prisoners starve
Cooties in jail
Doctor does not charge
At crossroad go this way
Hobos arrested on sight
Don't give up

ROAD SIGNS AND HOBO MARKS

PART ONE

Home always beyond the next curve in the road...

SONG FOR THE ROAD

A good traveler has no fixed plans
and is not intent on arriving.
                    Lao-Tzu

Travelers tote a portable definition
of home. It is scribbled in the dust
of the road, embedded in light
that slants through shuttered forests,
and comes unbidden in the call
of a distant train.

It quivers just beyond
the next expectation, shimmers
over the river's smocked surface,
unspooling down a mountainside
under a mood of clouds.

Caught in the reflective flash
of city windows and a skyline etched
against a setting sun,

it is chalked in alleyways,
and on the gatepost of a stranger's
rural home.

Sojourners adopt the comfort
of the road, the communal warmth
of campfire, while on a bosky hillside

the red-eyed towhee scruffs up the earth,
a primal dance, as if worshipping
the thrill of an ancient flame.

THE GREAT DEPRESSION

President Hoover says, *About the time*
we think we can make ends meet,
someone moves the ends.

Faces lined with hopelessness,
an unfamiliar scrawl that connects
men gathered around a soup kettle.
Tattered kids roll a discarded tire rim
down a dusty road; a woman slumps
on the curb, head cupped in her hands.

Marchers carry signs, *We want to be citizens*
not transients. Woody Guthrie sings,
Going Down the Road Feeling Bad.

These flinty people somehow
pull themselves up, in spite of despair,
the way some save tiny pieces of string,
tie the pieces together to make
something useful.

HOBO PRIDE

Like a dousing stick that seeks water,
a hobo rides the rails to find work,

unlike the tramp who travels and works
only when forced to do so

or the bum who does not travel
and does not work.

Their glyphs, a uniform code chalked
on light poles and fence posts,

aid those who follow: where to find
clean water, safe lodging, a kind heart.

They meet every August in Britt, Iowa, a family
of travelers who speak the same language.

Musicians and storytellers gather around
a common fire, celebrate their oneness.

The poets among them understand
how the mouth of night exhales its vapors

and how frost makes the dahlia beautiful
before it dies.

MEANING OF A NAME

Some choose a life on the road,
for others no luxury of choice.
Oldest son in a Depression family,
too many mouths to feed,
sent off to his fate on the road.

This boy of twelve, skinny child,
homeless boy — *a hobo*, stares
into the ominous face of survival.

There is no point for me to pivot on,
so protected my entire life.
I can't hear the crunch of the road,
the rumble of an empty belly.

What of this child? My imaginings
leave him scuffing down the road,
drinking from a spring
of disappointment, hungry always
for the warmth of a kitchen,
the shelter of familiar arms.

He will stake a claim to independence,
wade through need to grasp
a hand of goodwill,
learn a new language
of aloneness.

SHELTER

We can only know
the truth of our own story.

I have not traveled the boulevards
of your desires, been seduced

by the rhythm of wheels on rails,
or the murmur of a dark river.

Home always beyond
the next curve in the road

and work what you find,
where you find it.

I can imagine the comfort
of this symbol: two wavy lines

supported by a straight, vertical stroke,
a small circle sheltered underneath.

Rest in a barn loft filled with fresh hay
that smells of summer.

Hear rain's patter, watch lightning
flash through cracks in the walls.

The cows have been milked,
now quiet in their stalls.

Their breath warms the space
with a grassy vapor.

Morning opens to pale washed light
and the rooster's fanatical gladness.

Now cow bells and the clanking
of milk pails — a brief contentment.

A barn cat curls at your feet wanting
only the comfort of a warm body.

COMING TO TERMS

Four straight horizontal lines, nothing
in between, like garden rows free of weeds.

A spade, a rake exchanged
for a spoon and fork.

Housewife Feeds for Chores.
Is it right to expect something

in return? Were chores offered
with bread on a plate of respect?

Such a delicate thing, like trying to find
a splinter in a calloused hand.

The traveler will split, chop, and stack
the wood, enough to keep the flame going.

A woodpile in exchange
for rabbit stew.

THE TABLE

Two angled lines supporting
a longer horizontal stroke: *sit to feed*
promises more than a sandwich
handed out the door.

Perhaps a tablecloth, a candle,
flowers on the table. A blessing
or burden? Remove hat, spread
a napkin across lap.

And what of conversation
at this intersection where wanderer
and home folks meet? A curious
outpouring, so like a river,
confined within its banks, seeks
the release of sea.

Met up with my old friend 'Bo a few
weeks back. Turned into a rum dum.
Sky pilot couldn't save him.
Heard he flipped and missed. Greased
the tracks, caught the westbound.

EXTENDED FAMILY

They always set an extra place at their dinner table
for drop-in friends or unexpected guests.

One afternoon, just before dinner, a man came by
asking if he could work for food.

My friend and the traveling man raked leaves
that littered the front yard.

Afterwards, clean up at the sink and an invitation
to dinner; the guest served first.

No prying, just everyday conversation.
As he put on his coat to leave, tears watered

the furrows of his weathered face. *Can't remember
when I've had a hot meal like that, let alone*

sat at a table with family. They never saw him again.
He came into their lives like the wild geese that signal

untamed change. We are attracted to their call,
and charmed by the rightness of their sure flight.

BINDLE STICK FAITH

A cross marks the spot:
Talk Religion Get Food.

Who talks? Who listens?
No one is an expert here.

Travelers know the hope
of the road, the centrality

of flame, how smoke vanishes,
but its fragrance lingers.

They know the blessing of sunlight
the forgiveness of water

the kindness and hatred
of strangers,

grace wrought of suffering
and the fellowship of the fallen.

This nourishment served to hobos
following a sermon —

They call it *angel food.*

HOBO WISDOM

Here a squiggly horizontal line
on the fence post where a *poor man* lives.

Further on, much the same mark,
on the corner of the house that belongs
to a *bad-tempered owner,*

except the squiggles are closer,
more intense and the mark is trapped
inside a rectangular box.

Etiquette of the road demands
that travelers bypass the man
who does not have enough to satisfy
his own hunger,

yet what to say of the angry man,
poor in spirit, who suffers
from undefined hunger?

His plight is like the bitterness
of dandelion tea steeped
over an open flame, sipped
from a metal cup.

CAMP HERE

The mark is made with a continuous
swoop of the hand. Down, across,
then up. U-shaped, it provides
protection on three sides
and an opening for escape.

Camp Here: a resting place
for travelers comfortable on the road,
but needing an exit plan.

There's not much we absolutely
have to do. We choose
to stay put, move forward
or retreat, which could simply mean
to go in a different direction.

How much thought do we give
to where we stop and set up camp?
If we notice, marks made
by those who have gone on before
may lead to a ring of congenial spirits
gathered around a flame,
bacon sizzling and spitting out
its tantalizing aroma,
pancakes waffling in the pan,
one side, then the other.

ON THE EDGE

Danger crouches in the corners of boxcars
and in the clattering space between wheels and track.

It escapes over the lip of a bottle
to the lips of a desperate wanderer,

snarls from the throats of *bone polishers*
and menacing, angry men.

It glints off the edge of a knife's blade,
skips along a pitchfork's tines.

Hobos, carrying only bindle sticks, face the hard
fist of winter, the searing slap of summer's temper.

Inhaling risks, they measure the next breath
as testament to another day.

Finally, in remembrance, hobos who carry on
tap their walking sticks on the gravestones

of those who have *caught the westbound.*

BURLAP

*Armbands made of burlap are worn by those
in attendance at a hobo memorial service.*

Not the patterned elegance of moiré
nor satin's ballroom glow.
Common and coarse as a charwoman's
hands or a line-dried towel.

Here the touch of a callused palm
caught in the feedbag's weave;
burlap raised to the horse's mouth
filled with the grain of truth.

Potatoes lifted from earth's dark closet
shed their dusty layers, hibernate
inside burlap's sturdy shelter.

Burlap belongs to rivers and fields
and everyday people. Tattered and earthy
it challenges our ideas of beauty and wraps
our roots in what is real.

MEASURING RISK

Who first tasted plants to learn if they were safe to eat
and how many died?

Animals seem to know. Deer avoid foxglove that can stop
a heart; shun narcissus, buttercups, and lily of the valley.

Who sampled mushrooms, declared
some gastronomic delicacies, others deadly?

Who first realized potatoes are toxic
when they turn green?

That mistletoe, the kissing plant, and fragile
bleeding hearts harbor death?

In matters of the heart, a hobo couple
carry rhubarb leaves at their wedding.

Both bride and groom throw the bitter, lethal leaves
into a fire to symbolize the letting go of bad things.

Never completely safe, trust clambers over risk
for a glimpse of the future.

THE BONE POLISHER

Bad Dog lives in our neighborhood.
That's his name: Bad Dog, a basset hound.

He's not bad, really, just kind of dumb.
My grandson and I installed a night vision camera

and placed piles of meat scraps, hoping to photograph
coyotes that hunt nightly in our fields.

In the morning a flashing red light indicates
photographs have been taken.

Captured on the camera: fifteen photos
of Bad Dog, eating all the meat.

Hobos need not worry about a threat
from Bad Dog. No need here to place a symbol,

that looks vaguely like teeth, to warn
followers of a *mean dog, a bone polisher.*

I wish only that my home be marked
with a smiling cat:

A kindhearted lady lives here.

RATING SYSTEM

It's not the big fella with a knife
fashioned from a toothbrush

or that you must pee, or worse,
in a bucket.

Not even the crazy neighbor
who insults your mother

or the red-necked sheriff
with the maniacal grin.

The sign for jail is always
four lines down, four lines across

a grid with symbols attached.
Good Clean Jail, Jail Filthy,

Jail Good, but Prisoners Starve.
It's the grid with the indefinable

oval object drawn at the top
which gives pause:

Cooties in Jail.

THE MEANING OF CIRCLES

Strange how in a hobo's world
a circle may represent money
or a person; the circle representing
a person usually smaller.

A face within a circle, situated
near a cross, signifies:
Doctor does not charge,
as if to place redemption
and healing in close proximity.

At an intersection, a circle
with a line extending beyond
its perimeter directs the traveler —
At crossroad go this way.

Overlapping circles, as in Venn's
Diagram, symbolize areas
of commonality, but in the language
of the road this symbol warns
of handcuffs: *Hobos arrested on sight.*

Two tangent circles:
Don't give up.

HARD SCRABBLE LIFE

Ruth Stone, 1915 - 2011

Ruth Stone stalks truth. She writes
of a hard scrabble life *stained with pokeberries.*
She lived on *greens and back-fat and biscuits.*

The closest I can get to that life is my recipe
for Hobo Bread, a concoction of farm ingredients
baked in tin cans as hobos did during the Depression.

Poet dear, I'm inspired by your gnarly hands
grubbing stumps off your back forty, how you would
run when the words came, back to the cabin

to catch them before they got away. You took them
as they were, in grimy overalls, dirt under
their fingernails, bruised and wounded.

The hobos would have loved you, sitting around
a campfire, chewing the fat, an unlikely queen
proffering such naked, elegant words.

DEAR 'BO

I don't think you wish for wings.
I imagine your footsteps find ease
in the permanence of earth,
gravel's crunch and the chuffing
sound of mud.

You persist in my mind and I,
like a Pileated Woodpecker, drum
my head against the questions
of your need.

The obvious: to go where there is work,
but what of the enchantment of the road?
Does it circulate in the pathways of your blood?
We all are born crying for release.
When did that become your urgent need?

I don't know when or where this will reach you.
In my dreams you are a sunflower growing wild
on a Nebraska prairie, then suddenly
you turn into a wolf with kind eyes.

THE SHAPE OF LONGING

In the round weight
of stone cupped within my hand,
dense black and smooth
as a devil's eye,

and there in the curve
of the gull's wing
as it angles into the bleak winter sky.

Its enigmatic silhouette
draws me to an improbable tryst —
a horizon that fades into night
or a sunrise that simmers beyond
mountains, concealing its source.

Why fill with the rumble of want,
like a vagabond who bundles
his belongings, not knowing
where to go?

THE CAREGIVER

When my son was in college he picked up a hobo
standing in the rain at the edge of the road.

This son, unable to ignore anyone in need, bundled
the shivering man and his crutches into the car

and took him home. After providing a hot shower
and fresh underwear, he soaped and lathered the man's face,

shaved off weeks of growth. He cleaned and dressed
the inflamed stump of the hobo's right leg.

Following supper, the guest bedded down on the couch,
sleeping as if guarded by angels.

Next morning, fitted with a warm winter coat,
the traveler took to the road once again.

Does he hear romance in the call of a distant train?
Is there always a destination or never?

Some know what they need to be happy,
others know what they need to survive.

ROAD SIGNS AND HOBO MARKS

I

How many signs have we missed
and where would we be if we had seen them?

Flares warning accident ahead, caution
and stops obvious to everyone but ourselves.

Arrows that point in opposite directions.
Starting out we venture along by touch and feel,

blind to who we are, what we need.
How could we know?

The young wander in a vast landscape of choice
not knowing they can choose.

II

Soothed by repetition, seasons signal
a certain comfort,

our shadows moving across the years
with the tilt and spin of the earth.

We live within boundaries of change
without rising to its freedoms,

the way pansies lift themselves up
after a sprinkling of water;

too many days knotted into a tangle
of habit and duty.

The silver glint of rain, a certain slant
of light, grasses dried by summer heat,

snowberries and rosehips
primed for celebration.

III

So many signs we miss in our short life span:
The imperceptible movement of glacial ice fields,

explosions and deaths of stars, fossils in eternal sleep.
The universe sings, our time too brief for its melodies

to resolve in a grand finale of understanding.

IV

Deer come daily to my door.
They talk with persuasive eyes.

I cut apples. They eat slices
from my hand. Their wildness

has marked my house
with a language of trust.

Here an easy touch,
sure to find a handout.

Aren't we all beggars?

PART TWO

It is not easy to walk alone in the country without musing upon something.

- Charles Dickens

CHIMACUM

Small community on the Olympic Peninsula

Somewhere a fire is burning.
Someone is tending the fire.

Someone is gathering eggs,
feeding the calves, mucking

out the barn, and near
the crossroads

someone bellies up
to the diner's counter

coffee sloshing over the rim
of an ironstone mug.

At the community center
squirrels nip cones from fir trees,

a woodland syncopation
that punctuates the rural stillness.

Everything seems to walk
on soundless feet.

A man moseys along the road
clutching a brown paper bag.

Ordinary, yet remarkable
how we trundle

along each day
balancing our ration

of simple joys,
quiet troubles.

WHAT SOME CALL WILD

Some called him wild
this young man who became
my father

Soon after graduation traveling north
to work and sluice what he could
of life in Alaskan gold fields

Honeysuckle spiraling
into the forest like wildfire
does not name its wildness

nor the Nootka rose
which spills sweet wine
from thicket into night air

even wild mustard
that prances along the fence line
blesses the goldfinch

How much of wildness
is exuberance
set free

I hear him in raindrops
that patter on the cabin roof
It sounds like laughter

FLIGHT PATH

I hear them before I see them,
raucous excitement coming out of the north

and I run out to witness dark approaching clouds
that splinter into familiar aerodynamic chevrons:

the wild geese, waves and waves of them,
cresting over the house toward the lake at dusk.

Is it their fidelity to the season that lifts us up
to meet them, as if we are being birthed

into new expectations? Maybe we don't need to know
of the magnetic pull that directs them toward the poles

or the landmarks they remember
from earlier journeys. I like the mystery;

stars beginning to prick the deep of night,
winged silhouettes against the full moon.

JOY

How else to describe
the old couple holding hands

as they jump from the dock
into the lake naked,

their saggy butts, flabby thighs
hallmarks of enduring survival.

I wish I had been closer
when they hit the water

to see the widening ripples, catch
a few drops from the exquisite

fountain their bodies birthed.

THE WAYFARER

I am curious to know more about you,
closed off as you are from the other

beachcombers exploring the shore.
You sit, observing, fortified with

a pack, walking stick, and hat,
as if you plan to travel.

How little you reveal. Do you hear
the sigh of unnamed longings?

Does your gaze rest in a cloud
of dreams?

You are a darkened sky above a pastel shore.
Perhaps it's true — we need to be alone

to find out who we are.

WELLINGTON ON STEVENS PASS

*March 1, 1910: ninety-seven passengers and railroad personnel
lost their lives in the worst railroad disaster in U.S. history.*

The Great Northern serpentines into the Cascades,
rising and tunneling toward the west coast.

On board a young man travels, request of his parents,
to mediate grief following the death of his wife,

his small child left behind in their care.
He wants only to return.

Two opposing attorneys, unknown to each other,
are bound for the Supreme Court in Olympia.

Another man, estranged from his wife, journeys
west toward reconciliation.

And a widow tends her three children,
having just buried their father —

the infant's greedy need of breast,
toddlers jumping on the green mohair seats.

The train ascends through evergreens crusted
with wings of snow, flakes glitter

in blue dusk, a ballet of ice
swirling in the engine's headlamps.

Passengers dine, they smoke, exchange stories,
soothed by the rhythmic sway of the coach

the steady click-click of wheels marking time
over steel connections.

They crest the summit, begin descent
until the storm's rage prevents further passage.

Four days, five nights stranded on the side
of the mountain; the mounting loft of snow

fierce wind, thunder and lightning — a white heat
that casts an eerie incandescent beauty over the scene.

That night as they sleep on crippled trains,
the mountain, burdened with incomprehensible

snow, loses its hold, blasts down
the incline; the roar descends

over grinding boulders, cracking ice fields,
the snap of evergreens. It fills each quiet breath.

Claiming everything in its path, the avalanche
stops only when there is no place left to go.

DESIGNS OF THE WILD

Fields of fresh snow unmarked
by travelers' prints, a blank page
where the wild will write their stories
and beyond the ice-glazed lake.

A heron, unable to fish, hunkers
down wrapped in the comfort
of its great wings like a buttoned-up
professor in a cardigan sweater,
its careful three-pronged steps
record the history of hunger.

The deer come, their delicate hoof prints
circle the apple trees then disappear
as they clear the pasture fence,

and struggle shapes a fearful pattern,
blooms like a poinsettia in the snow
where a coyote skulked
and pounced its way to survival.

Along the rimed ridges of the feeder,
the wren tats a lacy motif composed
by the necessity of its work.

Now my crude booted footsteps mar
the snowy glitter of this winter morning,
here among the elegant designs of the wild.

And the stillness asks: how deep
or superficial our wanderings
as we chronicle our stories
into a new year and how much
grace in our designs?

MOUNTAIN RETREAT

Outside my window a tamarack
in the dim light of October.
Well into its transformation,
golden needles cluster around the trunk
and radiate out to the still green
tips of branches.

Nature's renovation, this deciduous conifer,
for much of the year masquerading
as an evergreen, now a bright flame
in the midst of the forest.

We should not be surprised.
Patterns replicate in all of us
as we show each other who we are.
Why then are we so often startled
by what seems like sudden change —
how reality stripped of its pretenses
appears as something else.

NOTES FROM A RAIN FOREST

Olympic National Park

By the lake a finch snatches
a fallen crust of bread, pulls off a crumb,
places it in the mouth of his mate.
He repeats this once again.

These secrets of nature,
how they saturate the inner life,
fueled with contrasts and contradictions
too large to fit the tote of our understanding.

So many ways to be together and apart.
Simplicity is a black beetle that scuttles
off with another; same size, shape,
and shine.

And here, nestled in the moss of the rain forest,
Russla emetica, the sickener, the red-capped
mushroom erupting like passion; a challenge
of risk and beauty.

And what are we to make of the gigantic spruce
that spirals upward, the trunk compressing
under its own weight, eventually to fall,
exploding at the end of its journey.

One can get lost in a green mist
of riddles, the glory and vulnerability
of it all. It's like going so deep
into the forest you forget about sky.

MOON GLOW OF BONE

After Robert Wrigley

The skulls, the viscera, the carcasses
glide in on drays of grace

like articles of faith marking
the land, a drum beat

that steadies each step
through pasture and forest,

the thrum of wings
beating against uncertain air

a heightened spiral that ascends
and disappears like unnamed longing.

Is it the sculptural beauty of bones,
how they become as flutes

filled with light and air,
the elegant ridges and hollows

of a hare's skull bleached
by a common sun?

These charms of death that slip
from the bracelet of understanding.

If there is a good death it is here:
The Church of Omnivorous Light

where the wild gather after the hunters
depart; a voracious celebration,

they feed on the abundance of life
satiated on what is left, what has been.

WOODWORKER SPEAKS OF MARRIAGE

The forest opens into a clearing, sunlight
slanting down the deep furrows of ancient Sequoias,
giants rooted here since before the birth of Christ.

I once saw a wedged slice of redwood six feet to its point,
he says. Centuries of history marked in those rings,
a concealed clock chiming time:

Dark Ages, Renaissance, explosions of exploration,
plagues, forest fires, drought.
Beginning growth is rapid, rings widely spaced.

With age, growth slows, rings pressed tight
until there is almost no space and the grain
becomes fine, yet at the center, forever,

the heart remains soft.

FLAWS

First day of school and she didn't like it:
the hole at the upper right side of her desk.

She thought to ask for a replacement,
an unblemished place to work.

She wondered why someone had rubbed
the tip of a pencil, in this particular spot,

over and over again, burrowing
into the wood like a termite.

The hole was smooth and she found
that her finger fit perfectly

into the hollowed-out space.
It had the silky feel of the green blanket

she had slept with when she
was a baby.

Yes, maybe this could be her desk.
Not another one like it anywhere

and somehow it felt like home.

HOOKED

My grown son wants me to write a poem
for young boys about fishing, an activity
that does not resonate with me.

I don't know what enticed my son to get up
before dawn, grab a pole, and head for the creek
yet, years ago, this was a common occurrence.

Now he remembers the quiet mists of early morning,
the satisfying ritual of digging worms, of securing
a wiggly worm on the hook.

He recalls the accelerated beat of his heart when he felt
a tug on the line and how it didn't matter the size —
it's the idea that something is out there.

He describes the sweet fishy smell of his tackle box
and offers to let me sniff it so I can experience the fragrance
that, to him, must be like sniffing *Joy* by Jean Patou.

I remember when he was eight, fishing on the Skagit River
near Rockport. A salmon struck and as he reeled it in,
excitement overtook him.

He threw down his pole, splashed into the river
in a vain attempt to wrestle the fish to the bank
and into his creel.

Yes, this is a poem for a young boy about fishing,
the young boy within my grown son.

LOOKING BACK

After Robert Graves, The Face in the Mirror

I contemplate my mirrored face
and it's like returning to a hometown,
after a long time away, where everything
has changed, yet some things
are achingly familiar.

Gone, the childhood scar on my forehead
where a chickenpox vesicle blossomed.
Gone, the freckles once sun-scattered
like confetti across my nose. I've gained
laugh lines at the corners of my eyes
and a vertical frown line, sculpted
at the center of my brow, like the statue
of the soldier in the village square.

My eyes, neither brown nor green,
are hopeful, one pupil larger than the other
as if I'm surprised, but not really.
The mouth has a determined slant
like the hill at the end of main street
that can be dangerous when icy,
sheltered as it is by overhanging maples,
but dappled in sunlight most of the time.

It is a full face, rounded out and generous
like the silver shingled house on the corner,
hollyhocks growing along the fence;

a curious house where much happened,
the house I walked by every day as a child
and now can't quite remember
who lived there.

YELLOWSTONE PARK, 1948

Memory stalks the years,
a distant traveler scuffing up
the dust of nostalgia —
a handmade Indian doll,
scrolled silver belt buckle,
an Old West saloon,
lightning lassoing the night sky
and I a dusty ten-year-old,
in the back seat of the Plymouth.

That night scrubbed in an old iron tub,
Yardley's English Lavender Soap,
clean pajamas, I hear wind rumpling
the pines, cones plunking
on the shingled roof of the cabin,
smooth log walls, butterscotch gold,
and knots like owl's eyes that see
everything. I remember that night
settled deep in a feather bed,
the line-fresh memory
I've used to measure comfort
for over sixty years —

crisp white sheets.

BOY AND DOG

Bronze Sculptures, Georgia Gerber
Langley, Washington

He is just a boy, yet he speaks
the ancient language
of longing.

It is marrow-deep,
this mute helplessness
held fast and it will not

be fleshed out,
we who must name,
cannot name what we most desire;

kindled in the salt of each cell,
an extravagant flame,
that burns with an odd sort of pain.

The boy leans against the rail
above Saratoga Passage
looks to the Cascades,

to peaks that gnaw at the sky,
as if those silent mountains
comprehend the histories

of whirling planets,
distant stars, our present,
defenseless need.

The dog lies at the boy's feet.
Waits. The ball in his mouth
a sphere of anticipated joy.

COUNTERBALANCE

She said she could never have another dog,
so much pain when he died, but what is love
without risk?

I say it is fearsome.
This morning the apple tree droops
under the weight of its fruit

and storm clouds skim over the lake,
heavy and threatening, yet hear the musical
pattering of those first raindrops.

What we cherish is weighted with risk,
and love is funny that way, because
it is also the fulcrum that lifts the burden.

THE CARD PLAYERS

Oil on Canvas, Paul Cezanne
The Louvre, Paris

They face each other,
these two, study their cards.

The shuffle, the snap; decisions
pulled from a random hand.

How to take what's given,
make something of it.

Contemplation burns
like embers in the tall one's pipe.

The smell of it circles the bottle
of spirits centered between them.

The muscular one leans forward,
drenched with yellow light,

the other, contained
in violet shadow.

And their hats —
one rigid, the brim firm

and poised as a pool cue,
the other soft and battered.

It's like sliding a weight along
the bar of a scales, this composition

of balance. Hard to say who has
the upper hand.

FORT CASEY CAMPGROUND

Whidbey Island

They come to claim a piece of the rock, and some say peace,
for a day or a week; their travel trailers, motor homes,
and fifth wheels lumber around the campground
like covered wagons rounding up for the night.

They circle the fires of convenience and luxury,
satellite dishes aimed at the sky above Seattle.
Generators grumble, mocking the waves which refuse to argue,
only a gentle hiss as they slide over rocks, return to the sea.

Their rigs are labeled with hopes and expectations:
Adventurer, Road Ranger, Prowler, Camelot, Four Winds.
What will they find in the swoop of an eagle
as it lifts a sequined salmon from the teal water

or the sight of eight herons circling like ancient spirits
coming to roost in the evergreens that ring the harbor,
and near the rocks, chancing upon a sea urchin
cracked open to reveal pink cathedral arches?

I walk each morning through the campground and muse
about the lives of these travelers, those who erect mesh fences
around their clutch of land and those who bring tents,
sleep close to the earth. I like to think about what brings

them joy and why, but mostly I love the smell
of their breakfast bacon.

THE STORYTELLER

He hears voices. They are coming from the attic
above his workshop.

Until this intrusion, retirement allowed him
the luxury of a workshop retreat: comfortable chairs
around a wood burning stove, tools and equipment
neatly arranged, and a TV suspended on cables,
that could be raised or lowered by remote control.
(He says the TV sometimes moves up and down
of its own accord.)

He climbs into the attic thinking the voices
may come from homeless persons who have found
a warm place to sleep, but finds no signs of habitation.

This has gone on, intermittently, for weeks.
His wife, not quite a non-believer, is beginning
to tip-toe in that direction. The man a bit mystified,
but in good humor, likes to tell the story
to old friends who stop by, his smile a slice of slyness.

Now his wife's computer is on the fritz. Out comes
a guy from Comcast. After solving the computer
problems, as he passes by the workshop, he says,
"What's that I hear?" The man's surprised reply:
"Oh, you hear it too?"

Clutching sanity close to his chest,
he learns that Navy jets, flying overhead

in scheduled patterns, have been communicating
with the TV, turning it on and off, raising
and lowering it at random times.

It was an intriguing story while it lasted.

THE CIDER PRESS

Two old guys, they speak a common
language, a comfortable back and forth,
sprinkled lavishly with references
to cranks, and screws, hinges, and pulleys,
spindles, and chutes, levers that lift
and pull and open; an intimacy evolved
from growing up on farms
where what you need is in a distant town
and *make-do* is how it was.

One has built a cider press, a beautiful
wooden press which would fit agreeably
in an art gallery. The two peruse the project:
the aged oak frame salvaged from the local dump
before recycling became a trendy option,
and slatted squeezing barrels constructed
from the same salvage. The brass
toilet seat hinge attached to the lid over
the apple hopper; the hopper sealed
with beeswax. A washing machine motor
and pulleys that power the grinder, and shredders
that once were hack saw blades. Lawn mower
wheels make the cider press portable.

An extra wheel, *like a fly wheel,* keeps
the press running at a steady pace
and last autumn one hundred forty-nine
gallons of sweet cider flowed from
that press, a wonder of ingenuity
and compression.

MOUNTAIN MAN IN TIE AND WHITE JACKET

For Bob

My dentist pans for gold.
In Montana, at six thousand feet,
he digs, sifting through granite
and flint; trinkets of millennia,
alert to that mineralized vein
burnished in the stream
of his dreams, the one that,
surprisingly, does not glitter.

Fools gold, he says
when I bring him a twinkling
stone from my garden and then,
sweet man that he is, smiles,
*Interesting rock to come from
an island.*

He may have packed more gold
into the molars of his patients
than he has packed out
of those hills, but I think
he hankers for Townsend,
that little town where friends
wave and wear cowboy hats,
as he grinds and picks
in the hollow of my tooth;
sluices my mouth with water.

A CURIOUS LIGHT

The storm is coming; wind out of the south
shouting its way up the inlet causing waves
to bare their teeth.

Seven herons leave the fury near shore,
land into the wind, evenly spaced across our field.
They move as one in the same direction,

stealthy seekers on a search and destroy mission.
Some storms give us time to prepare, others hit
without notice, buffet us like a broken promise.

Living on an island teaches us to do without:
not only designer clothes and French wines,
occasionally milk and bacon.

When the storm takes out our power
for days and days, we burrow
into our homes like small animals, seek

the comfort of candles, blankets, and books;
clutch hot water bottles, spin fantasies of summer.
Camping near the fireplace, flames throw shadows

against the walls, illuminate a favorite photo:
Forgotten Homes. A deserted house stands alone
on a prairie under a dark sky filled with the brilliance

of stars, a snowy mountain in the distance.
Walls canted, doors and windows gone,
yet a curious light shines through holes

in the roof and escapes doorways,
as if the house, abandoned and battered
by elements and time, has held on

to the glow of home.

VOICES

The ancients tell us sheep follow the shepherd
because they know his voice.

The voice of the wind is familiar, yet unreliable,
as are the syllables of the sea.

And trees have their own language which can comfort
or intimidate depending on how they argue with the wind.

Calmed by a mother's voice, a child claims an ancient bond
of sound waves through fluid, blood through a cord.

The voice of reason rings ancient bells that chime
through venerable halls of wisdom to our best instincts.

The voice of silence is dependable, as is the space between
words, the space between musical notes. We come to rest

in the expanse of silence. Somehow, I find my way.
Stumble and fall. Find voices I trust and a voice I place on paper.

I like what the Irish say about trust: *You are the place I stand
on the day when my feet are sore.*

Note: *Translation of quote by Paraig O Tuama*

SOURDOUGH

The Jesuit baker, Brother Curry, says
capture wild yeast.

 A net? A trap? Kind words?
Just a bit of flour, warm potato water

and a little honey. Cover loosely.
Three days later

a bubbling, frothing cauldron;
a spongy, ever-shifting mass.

No eye of the newt or toe of frog,
wool of bat, tongue of dog.

Some would say pure chemistry,
yet like an ordinary life

that holds its secrets, I like to think
how sweetness nourishes the cells,

the hidden fermentation that brings
about change, the magic of transformation.

My floured hands knead the dough
in praise of air and lightness

and rising.

THE SUM OF THEIR WORK

Honeybees travel to find work,
dozens of them among the flowers,
humming their satisfied tune;
like fat bankers in pinstripe suits
they collect their payments.

I sit in the garden, watch
their industrious ways,
wonder what they have chosen
as a vessel for their liquid asset,
where is the repository
for their gold.

In one lifetime
can we ever hope
to invest so wisely?

DRIFT

Not all those who wander are lost.
J.R.R. Tolkien

A foggy morning at the shore;
a heron ghosts out of the mist
floating by on a slim raft of driftwood.

Did dense clouds at the heights
force him to find another way to travel?
This elegant, yet comic, mariner

abandons himself to the wind
and tides, an inventive flight
over water.

Slow ease, perfect balance, deviation
from the norm: a fearless artist
creating a unique design.

Sunlight shimmers through the fog
defying sharp boundaries; a soft blend
of unexpected shapes, unplanned course.

At times we need to drift
to clear our vision. We don't know
what we'll find until we wander.

GLOSSARY

Angel Food: Food given following a sermon.

'Bo: Name hobos call each other.

Bone Polisher: Mean dog.

Caught the Westbound: To die.

Flip: Jump on a train.

Greased the Tracks: Hit by a train.

Hobo: A homeless person who travels to find work.

Rum Dum: A drunk.

Sky Pilot: A preacher.

ABOUT THE AUTHOR

Lois Parker Edstrom, a retired nurse, is the author of five collections of poetry. *What Brings Us to Water* won the 2010 Poetica Publishing Chapbook Award. *What's To Be Done With Beauty* received the Creative Justice Award in 2012. *Night Beyond Black* was published by MoonPath Press in 2016, and *Glint,* MoonPath Press, 2019. *Road Signs and Hobo Marks* is her third full-length book.

She has received two Hackney National Literary Awards, the Outrider Press Grand Prize, and the Westmoreland Award. Her poems have appeared in literary journals such as *Clackamas Literary Review, Floating Bridge Review, Rock & Sling, Mobius,* and *Adanna.* Edstrom's work has received nominations for a Pushcart Prize and the Washington State Book Award.

Three of her poems have been read by Garrison Keillor on *The Writer's Almanac,* and her poetry has been featured in *American Life in Poetry.* In 2016 Edstrom's career in nursing and her poetic passion coalesced when her poem, *Choices We Make When We Are Too Young to Make Them,* appeared in *Poems in the Waiting Room,* a publication furnished to hospitals and to doctors' offices in New Zealand. Her poetry has been translated into Braille, and has also been adapted to dance by the Bellingham Repertory Dance Company. The natural beauty of Whidbey Island, where she lives with her husband, inspires much of her work.